The non-obvious explosive ideas tha

Sharp, articulate, and immediately useful

Most Businesses struggle to find leads and achieve sales because they often talk to the wrong audience for their offerings.

Clickbait marketing is used to little effect because business owners tend to copy what their competitors are doing. It is not your fault business owners, you have been told to do so. To get ideas from the competition that inspires you but is rather predictable.

The non-obvious explosive ideas that work content give you great ideas that work because, in many ways, it is the opposite of the traditional lead generation strategy. Rather than creating a few highly academic and technical reports and forcing people to render their email addresses for the purpose of leads generation, The non-obvious Marketing wheels drive brands to think like Apple—find something useful to say to your audience, and offer it freely in a way that is interesting to people far outside your industry and causing them to purchase and repurchase your goods and services.

This is a book about learning the theories that predict your future sales. Most life decisions arrive in short-term rational thought processes. Often decisions are made through an emotional lens. People buying decision are often biased and does not make much sense on the offset, however, it offers a solution to their problem satisfying a need.

In a world where big data is the driver and everyone is one click away from being a self-declared marketing expert, learning to think differently is more important than ever. Observing and curating ideas using the marketing wheel can lead to a unique understanding of why people buy, sell, or believe anything.

Customer acquisition is mighty important in your business and my philosophical theory is to collect ideas the way frequent buyers collect Fribiz—as momentary rewards to use for later redemption. I introduce to you the Customer Acquisition theory of relevance equivalence $C=NC2$.

The Theory of Relativity in Marketing

E=MC2
Albert did this the theory of relativity — Physics

C=NC2
Trisha did this the theory of relativity — Marketing

C means Customers
N means Niche 80% of what you do 20% of people relate to it in any industry.

C means Conversion - 20% of your audience buying your products or services in any industry.

Scan to continue

The Manual for SME

x2 repeated purchases of your products & services by 20% of your audience in any industry.

Why I wrote The Customer Acquisition theory of relativity

When I started writing my first theory, I did not know that it would turn into a list of concepts in 2018. I intended to share strategic ideas and methodologies that work that have a home with any project because they are working in the background.

All my terrific brainstorming theory models came to me in my hot bath water because I like to meditate in my hot bath water, and ideas formed in my head that I write on my bathroom ceramic tiles with my wet finger.

In 2018, the first conceptual hypothesis about Competitor Analysis expanded beyond the trends that big data presented to feature an inside look at my process for managing competitors in a way that engenders partnership in your business as opposed to competitors' rivalry.

I introduce to you Girlfridayz's Road Block Competitors Analysis model.

Girlfridayz - Girlfridayz's Road Block Analysis

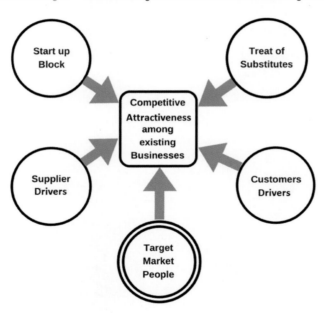

Why Most Competitor Rivalry Are Spectacularly Useless

In 1979 Porter's five forces analysis framework was first published in Harvard Business Review. The five forces analysis presented a method of analysing the operational environment of competition in a business.

We found that Porter's five forces analysis framework presents the more "hostile" side of the competition of a business— rather unattractive and encouraging rivalries among companies.

If you consider the number of businesses that any one of us is exposed to on an average day, the quest to find customers amid the noise is a challenge we all know personally. Girlfridayz Road Block Analysis helps you navigate information overload and join the competition offering partnership rather than useless rivalry that caused misery. Our framework competitor analysis operational model offers a much better approach to competitors analysis and encourages enterprises' partnership.

Are you a business owner that goes to PLAY in the PARK with a SCARF on?

The great neuroscientist David Rock created the SCARF Model

Meaning as people we all love

1. Status
2. Certainty
3. Automony
4. Readiness
5. Fairness

The great behavioural psychological marketer Trisha Amable CEO of Girlfridayz Limited created PLAY in the PARK model®

PLAY

1. Plan
2. Long-Term
3. Activities
4. Yearly

in the **PARK**
1. Productive
2. Achievable
3. Relatable
4. Keen

In Business to **PLAY in the PARK**® created by Trisha Amable CEO of Girlfridayz on 10/02/2023 informed you that you need a SCARF because you don't want to be left out in the cold as we prefer to be warm and have lots of friends to buy from within a friendly trustworthy environment.

Hence forming partnerships in business encourages long-term planning to acquire customers and ultimately increase the business's profitability. In business strategic planning is an important part of the tactical plan of your company and I am introducing Girlfridayz- Gap Reduction Strategic Action Model created on 06-04-2019.

Girlfridayz - Gap Reduction Strategic Action

Structure

Long-Term Goals

GAP Analysis Reduction Strategy

Actions

Resources

Strategic Planning

Your Internal Resistance to Change

The Underappreciated Side Of Data

How can collecting ideas —becoming the recipient for developing genuine insight can give you firsthand research, survey and focus group to curate the best ideas for products or services development?

Why it is easy to assume that data means entering numbers into a spreadsheet or referencing some piece of analytics published in a Marketing and Business journal—the truth is, data has a forgotten side that has little to do with experimenting and far more rely on your power of observation.

When you think of the science and discipline that goes into product development and manufacturing as well as services development attracting professionals or individuals to your website or brick-and-mortar, a complex step-by-step methodology is used to achieve the desired outcome. I am introducing to you the Products and Services Matrix.

Product Type

The type and kind of product introduce to the market

Matrix

Product Design

Product plan including mechanism, branding, and design

Service Type

The type of service introduce to the market

Matrix

Service Branding

Service name and branding of the service

Girlfridayz Product Development

Girlfridayz Service Development

Product Prototype

Full product designed with mechanism fully working

Matrix

Product Production

Manufacturing of the final working product

Service Development

Offer of the service and how it's presented

Matrix

Service Presentation

Presentation of the service either online or offline

When you think about the discipline that goes into product manufacturing research to produce raw data, experimentation, and testing can seem like a task only performed by robotic perfectionists still require a method. The truth of studying products or services development without the matrix might not be accurate.

When creating products or purchasing products to sell you need to purchase or create them with your audience in mind. The same goes for the creation of your service you need to create them with your audience in mind because we can make something that people need or create something that we think people need and persuade them to buy.

You need to relate to your audience before you could sell anything because the side hustle offers something worth much more than money —a hedge against feeling stuck and dull, cheated by life, your customers, and prospects will turn to your business for a solution to their problem. In the best-case scenario, your side hustle can be like offering your services or products as a solution.

You might just hit the jackpot and discover that holy as it might be your customers might not be ideal to deal with and require more information on your products or services. Your role is to assess the need by using The Star Sales Principales and start selling like a pro, ascertaining the situation, task, action and result obtained for the customers' satisfaction. I introduce to you The Sales STAR Principales strategy created on 13-04-2019.

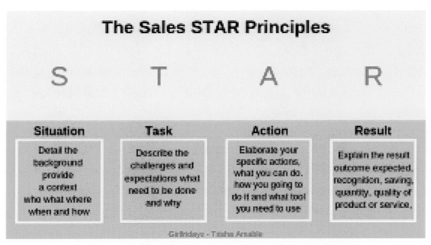

The Sales STAR Principles

S   T   A   R

Situation	Task	Action	Result
Detail the background provide a context who what where when and how	Describe the challenges and expectations what need to be done and why	Elaborate your specific actions, what you can do, how you going to do it and what tool you need to use	Explain the result outcome expected, recognition, saving, quantity, quality of product or service,

Girlfridays - Tisha Amalie

I wish I learned this earlier before starting an upward trend in sales and profit margins. Because I recognised in 2019 that my movement needed to do more than repeat common knowledge to fool customers into purchasing our services. It was not really "fooling" but I was assuming that everyone is responding to the same stimulus which was a resounding error in behavioural psychological connotations.

I was not objective trying to sell website design to someone insecure, declaring 2019 the "Year of Makeover Or You're out" is clearly self-serving. Of course, most bias is not visible to the receiver and works miracle and objectivity became notoriously difficult for some of my customers who require clarity.

I had no insight because trends need to do more than repeat common knowledge. I mean saying that "More people will buy products or services from upgraded website content" is obvious—and useless, because it lacks insight. This was me lazy thinking because it was easier to do than offering an informed and insightful point of view. Why has nobody told me this before? I needed to find out and I did.

What I have learned that great trends are unexpected, unpredictable instead, they share new ideas in insightful ways while also describing the accelerating present situation your customers faces.

I had no proof— what I mean by this is 2019 —sharing a trend without specific examples is like declaring that you are the captain of a boat after having taken a few lessons or measuring your business input without the correct method you are sure to fail like going boating and sailing without a plan because you have declared yourself a captain.

Exceptional examples and stories are powerful components of illustrating why evergreen content matters. They are necessary processes for proving your credibility because finding just one example and declaring something a trend without more evidence is usually guesswork.

Perhaps the most common area where many business owners' trend predictions fall short is in the discussion of the problem with their customers. It's not enough to think about the customer's problem in the context of describing them as your own problem, the best way to answer the customer's problem contextually forecast go further than just describing what's happening without the solution in mind.

Why we developed The Star Sales Principles —Sales like a seasoned pro is because, at the start of my business, I was looking for Marketing strategies that work and was presented with clickbait headlines similar to New Year's resolution to lose the weight gained of Christmas past. Unfortunately, the side-effect on consumers is nobody sticks to all these fad diets presentations as they are not encouraging but sound good off the bat.

Here are a few of the worst-offending, most obvious 'trends' I've seen:
- "It's all about the visuals."
- "Streaming video content."
- The Year of Drones has arrived. Really"
- "Content marketing will continue to be the place to be."
- "Fantasy sports."

These should not be described as trends. Some are just random buzzwords or the name of platforms not inspiring to anyone and without context, they are just flat and meaningless and don't fit the description of a unique idea describing the accelerating present.

Great introspection is never an obvious declaration of facts that most people already know. Instead, quiet introspection can be extremely valuable because they share new ideas in insightful ways describing the accelerating present we found ourselves in. The Non-Obvious Explosive Ideas That Work focus on the intersection and introspection of multiple consumers' behaviour and beliefs describe below. I introduce to you Girlfridayz's psychological model of consumers' wants and needs.

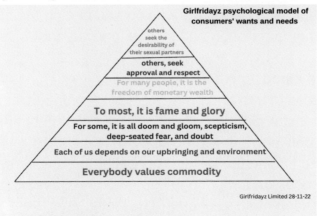

Girlfridayz psychological model of consumers' wants and needs

others seek the desirability of their sexual partners

others, seek approval and respect

For many people, it is the freedom of monetary wealth

To most, it is fame and glory

For some, it is all doom and gloom, scepticism, deep-seated fear, and doubt

Each of us depends on our upbringing and environment

Everybody values commodity

Girlfridayz Limited 28-11-22

Over the next few pages, you'll learn a step-by-step technique that can support you in thinking differently about customer acquisition relevancy (C=NC2), escaping the self-delusion that you're not enough and that's ok as long as you are willing to escape from toxic clickbait environment that leads to obvious lazy thinking ideas.

In doing so, you'll immediately feel liberated and free because of having more insights than your peers around you and seeing the connections between customer acquisition and stories in a way that most people don't.

The key to the method you're about to learn is a willingness to go outside your usual sources of info and open your mind to unconventional ways of thinking and brainstorming. As a result, you'll become better at spotting the connection between The Core Assets + The Cellar: A Winners Combination and finding the key to The Cellar the online resources attached to the book and the things you read that have no relevance to the customer acquisition method used in The Cellar and The Core Assets.

There's an alchemy to be found in thinking like a trend curator. Let's talk about how I found it.

Across decades of observation of vulnerable people in society, interviewing customers, working with professionals, lawyers, doctors, psychiatrists, and other professionals, as well as observing my colleagues at work and outside work allowed me to develop an elegant pyramid to describe in seven levels why some people are more susceptible than other responding to different stimulus and likely to be influenced by cleverly crafted marketing technic. Girlfridayz's psychological model of consumers' wants and needs— is the perfect representation of consumer behaviours.

The consumers' wants and needs describe why some people manage to exceed their potential while others peak early or never achieve the same success. I have found over the year that it all depends on your mindset. People with fixed mindsets believe that their skills and abilities are set and tend to think rather in a binary fashion whether they are good at something or not good at something.

Therefore, the latter tend to focus their efforts on tasks and in their careers where they feel they have a natural ability.

People with growth mindsets believe that success and achievement—are the results of hard work and grit. They see their own and others' true potential as something to be proud of and defined through effort and come with a passion for learning and love & thrive on challenges.

When it come to setbacks, people react differently.

When it comes to setbacks, people with a growth mindset tends to treat failures and setbacks as minor inconvenience until a solution is found by looking for a suitable solution to the problem that will change the outcome. They are more resilient, have more self-confidence, and are less focused on getting revenge for any perceived wrong like a person with a fixed mindset that will put the blame on someone else as opposed to assuming responsibility and accountability for their failures and setbacks. People with a growth mindset tend to be happier than fixed mindset people.

Despite many benefits of adopting a growth mindset, the sad reality is that each of us depends on our upbringing and environment. As soon as we can evaluate ourselves and our personal goals, we develop behaviour and habits towards it. For most people, it is the fame and glory that matter most, and for many people, it is the freedom of monetary wealth the driver. Others seek the approval and respect of others. For some people, it is the desirability of their sexual partners that matter most.

However, it is not because you have a growth mindset or a fixed mindset that you don't display these behavioural traits—for some people, it's all doom and gloom, deep-seated fears, and doubt—a limitation that will continue to impose unaware behavioural characteristics upon the sufferer. However, everybody values commodities.

The Girlfridayz's psychological model of consumers' wants and needs describes Abraham Maslow's simple psychological Hierarchy of needs self-realisation.

The highest level of his pyramid of our basic needs is self-realisation. Our psychological consumers' model of wants and needs represents the desire to become the most that one can be —including behavioural traits brought on by personal goals attainment and the development of characteristics due to imposing limitations on oneself regardless of the cultivated mindset of the consumer.

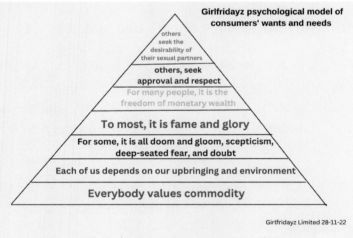

Girlfridayz psychological model of consumers' wants and needs

others seek the desirability of their sexual partners

others, seek approval and respect

For many people, it is the freedom of monetary wealth

To most, it is fame and glory

For some, it is all doom and gloom, scepticism, deep-seated fear, and doubt

Each of us depends on our upbringing and environment

Everybody values commodity

Girlfridayz Limited 28-11-22

Pay attention to the world, and train yourself to notice the details that others miss. Don't listen to the haters. These people are the background noise of insecurities talking and see a potential in you that they want to kill before you can do anything meaningful in society and serve your relatable audience. When you want to startups a business, the latter is of utmost importance to follow because you never start otherwise.

Take back your power, embrace your talent and natural abilities, face your fears and train your brain for happiness and success by developing a growth mindset because you will automatically gain a positive attitude towards life and your business dealing, achieving your business goals and plan for long-term gain & profitability.

Sometimes in business, we don't like doing something, however, it is a necessary step for business growth purposes and customer acquisition. Therefore, learning to relate to your audience is a must to achieve abundant monthly sales in your business, and repeated purchases are a must for business sustainability as well as gaining new customers, prospective leads and enquiries. I introduce to you The Audience Attraction Matrix.

Girlfridayz
Leads and sales strategic matrix®

Right Audience

Wrong Audience

Existing Market

New Market

Leads and clients acquisition

on the off chance to get a lead or client

TARGET MARKET

on the off chance to get a lead or client

Leads and clients acquisition

How to nurture your audience with relatable content that eventually leads to sales or enquiries.

In 2015, I started writing my business and marketing blog, I decide that I will talk about every area of a business's internal and external processes and customer acquisition. I decided not to allow comments on my business blog.

Forwarding to 2023 we have achieved our goal. Our business blog has over 200 articles about business and marketing and it's read by 1700 people on average per month. Google ranked our business blog post article, and we have achieved page authority/ page rank and domain authority for some popular articles like The Importance of A PESTEL Analysis which has 14,707 views and 19 likes and was written in 2018.

Because of the popularity of our business blog, we are receiving requests from other bloggers to link articles or guest blogging that we don't allow. You can advertise your products or services in any of our blog posts for a token fee, and your adverts will be clicked on due to our high ranking on Google and people reading our blog post article.

Take the time to reflect on your viewpoint before sharing it in a considered manner

In 1982, a book called Megatrends changed the way governments, businesses and people thought about the future. The author John Naisbitt predicted our evolution from an industrial society to an information society, and he did so more than a decade before the advancement of the internet as we know it. He predicted the shit from hierarchies structure to network, and the rise of global economy.

John Naisbitt was, and still is at 90 years old a collector of ideas. For years, his ideology has inspired me to think about the world with a similar broad lens and helped me to develop the process that I use in my own online business Girlfridayz Limited (website) and my work, which I called **spotting opportunities that others don't see.**

In 2022 after listening to Rory Sutherland, Vice Chairman of Ogilvy about choice architecture and other psychological effect people respond to. We created a butterfly effect on Girlfridayz.com by changing our website's presentation of our order forms and buttons on our website as well as introducing a choice architecture for our website design offers—
all-inclusive Bundles for your site and the budget website offer —add more pages; you're in control, worked a treat with our website visitors.

These small changes to our website presentation on some pages, forms and buttons caused an unpredictable beneficial effect on our sales which increased by 98% overnight, generating about £15806 sales per month on a good month and a bad month £5897 sales increasing.

In the next pages we will details exactly how this beneficial change to our website caused a mega unpredictable effect by observing and listening to Rory Sutherland YouTube videos mainly about marketing and advertising discussing behavioural science and psychology marketing.

I learned early a true story of how the butterfly effect in psychology works and increased Best Buy e-commerce website sales by $3000000 just by changing the checkout button to continue and a small message saying you don't have to register your details to shop with us, however, for future speedy checkout you can register an account. Previously their checkout button said to register an account before they could check out putting off visitors.

In 2022, I watched Rory on YouTube and listened to him inspire me to make changes to my website for the better. The idea was that we would help our customers and remove what could put them off and bounce.

The improvements made were small but mighty. We reversed the order of choice on our online order form by adding a header message and small fun messages in between the option of services offered as if you are walking in the hall of your favourite supermarket viewing all the optional services choices for your start-up and SME experiencing The Services Buying Customer Journey on Girlfridayz.

Our online form improvement aimed to help brands work with influential —
messages to boost sales of our services for startups and SMEs.

There was no problem with this well-intentioned plan—none of us knew
about its butterfly effect on our customer acquisition.

Further online form development underwent, and we added the upload of
documents and images option. The purpose was to facilitate the upload of
customers' information for our CV services and graphic design advertising
services—saving time because the customer no longer needed to email
their details to us as they can upload their information straight from the
online order form.

The non-obvious idea was to remove the added stress customers might
feel filling out an online order form.

The online order form captures the customer's details last because it feels
like a natural step to complete their order reducing the opportunity to
bounce off and increasing the happiness level.

Those improvements to our website include changing all the buttons of our choice architecture of services on every page to "continue"—Is a call to action that feels natural at the end of a powerful message about our services offered. I am introducing to you The 5 Sales Drivers and The 4 Complimentary Sales Drivers.

Girlfridayz 5 Sales Drivers ®
Audience Attraction Sales Drivers Matrix

TM - Target Market
Who's your audience and how do you relate to your audience.

RW - Reason Why
Your purpose for contacting your prospects or customers.

H - Headline
How do you attract your audience.

D - Differentiation
How do you differentiate your products or services.

FB - Products & Services Benefit and Features.

Girlfridayz 4 Sales Drivers ®
Audience Attraction complimentary Drivers Matrix

TM - Target Market
Who's your audience and how do you relate to your audience.

G - Guarantee
A promise with certainty that you will do what you prescribe.

IO - Irresistible Offer
A tempting offer to attract prospects.

CTA - Call to action
Short powerful text for prospects to act on content.

SP - Social Proof
Review by customers or prospects

Gathering is the disciplined act of collecting stories and ideas from reading, listening, and speaking to different sources.

The Cellar is a collection of stories and ideas you can use in your business to grow. Because it incorporates the disciplined act of learning from various sources—reading, listening, viewing media and using tools to progress your learning journey. The Cellar online resources attached to The Core Assets + The Cellar: A winners Combination and The Core Assets of Marketing With its Dual Implementation Support System - The Cellar are your personal development tools through the discipline of reading, listening, viewing media, using tools collecting ideas on your way from different sources to increase your business dealing and customer acquisition.

Those first seven years of building the foundation of our business Girlfridayz Limited took us on a learning journey about business.

My point in sharing this story is to illustrate how the pressure to find enough ideas worth writing about on my business blog and website helped me get better at saving and sharing ideas (my business tools calculators) that my customers and prospects cared about.

My method involves always writing in a notebook my ideas and keeping them on my desk for easy retrieval. Here's how I keep my notebook notes written on any piece of paper I find to jot down ideas quickly was organised. Big Ideas, Story, Trend, Book to read, Contact, Website update, Event to attend, Stastic, App Development, To Do List, People to meet.

Being organised and consistent increases my website views over time, customer acquisition, prospect enquiry and work testimonials placed on our website due to planning brand works excellently carried out. I am introducing to you The TIME Matrix—When it comes to qualifying leads — remember it's about time.

Girlfridayz's TIME Matrix®

When it comes to qualifying leads — remember it's about time

Timing

Iteration

Multiple

Engage®

Timing is concern with government influence, social trend, environmental influence and Customer needs.	Iteration is concern with the product's or service's content lifecycle and the customers, leads omnichannel, multichannel journey experience.	Multiple is concern with the multiplying effect of the strategy and tactics used in content strategy to attract the lead/customer to purchase from a business.	Engage is concern with the likelihood of the lead, customers engaging with a business content, purchasing product or service from a business and reviewing purchases.

Aggregating involves taking individuals' ideas and grouping them together to uncover bigger themes—The Complete Leads and Clents Enabler.

After gathering ideas, the next step is to combine the early result of my observation and curiosity with some insights about how my list of theories and ideas might fit together in the overall theme of customer acquisition, C=NC2

At this stage, a common trap to avoid when ideas come to you from different sources is to delay writing them down as soon as possible. Aim to aggregate based on insights and human motivations nudges stimuli that customers and prospects respond to—and achieve leads and sales using the marketing models, business models and analysis found in this book about customer acquisition deriving from reading, listening and speaking to different sources.

Elevating involves finding the underlying themes that connect groups of ideas to describe a single bigger concept.

If you've gone through gathering and aggregating ideas like we did? The point at which you'll derive from the solution to elevate your ideas into a single concept encompassing the ideas subset that is interesting to the users and feels significant for your customer acquisition following your intuition like we did at Girlfridayz.

Even though you might not be able to describe why this concept works— embrace that intuition, and start your own story. In later phases of The Girlfridayz Audience Attraction Matrix Complete, you can connect your customer's acquisition story and increase profitability to a broader idea.

How do you know what to focus on to build out a trend? The goal to achieve this third step— is to take a broader view and connect your smaller clusters of ideas into larger ones that describe huge and potentially more prevalent powerful ideas.

More than any other step, this is where the breakthroughs and inspiration come from my relaxing hot bath water. My relaxed mind drifts to my next big idea for customer acquisition. In this state of mind, I developed my last theory in 2023, C=NC2 —The Theory of Customer Acquisition Equivalent Relevancy in Marketing.

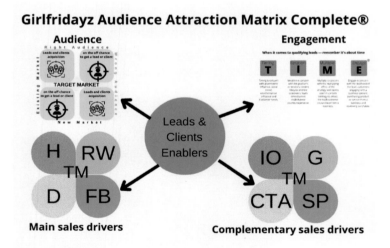

How to optimise your marketing

In writing the non-obvious explosive ideas that work, I recall interesting memories of how I started this hypothesis list for customer acquisition in 2018 and built on it to arrive at The Customer Acquisition Relevancy Equivalent theory —$C=NC2$ in 2023.

In this book, you'll find proof that ideas can come from anywhere and your brain can produce the next innovations in your business when you are in a relaxed environment.

My imagination enabled my creativity and my observation skill, strong intuition and a strong desire to be successful allows me to visually represent my early struggle in customer acquisition in my business. I developed 15 innovative marketing and business strategical models and analyses that support you to increase your customer acquisition using the right method. knowing what the consumers respond to and their susceptibility to cleverly crafted marketing messages and pictures can help you increase leads and sales for maximum profitability.

HOW TO OPTIMISE YOUR MARKETING

By Girlfridayz

the startup way

Your core product
You would want to sell it at is price value.

Create a lead magnet and a Tripwire

A low offer that is irresistible or offer a gift in exchange for email

show lead magnet and tripwire to many people

Automation
Upsell downsell-profit maximiser

find a person with a lot of money, an

investor

find a **influencer** who can share your product or recommend you

sell your product to million of people - email marketing - webinar - blog - Social Media - Advertising

list your company on business listing or stock exchange

like NASDAQ

your investor and you all make money when you

sell your core offer there

brought to you by : **Girlfridayz**

Girlfridayz provide you with the insight you need to optimise your marketing

http://girlfridayz.com

Naming is the creative art of describing a brand or products or services in an easily understandable and memorable branded way.

Naming a brand or service is a bit like naming a child— you think of every way that the name balances the connotation that feels right.

Naming a service or branding a service involves sharing a specific viewpoint that a service name conveys meaning to the service offer with simplicity—and they're often memorable. Because names often contain words and phrases that sell.

Why we at Girlfridayz named our services and our packages offer, in effect branded our services for immediate recognition, attracting leads, and prospects to our award-winning government-accredited services and helping us to achieve massive sales of our services to our audience startups and SMEs.

If you like this...

Consider purchasing these:

The concept for my other book, *Likeability* took off immediately. Because people understood the ideas within them and saw growth potential using the book with its attached mentoring online resources—quirky enough to inspire purchases in abundance. Finding the non-obvious explosive ideas that work can do that for you; as we did find out.

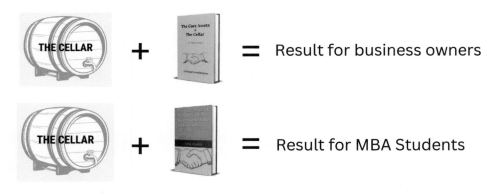

Scan to view our website and experience the
Service Buying Customer Journey

Printed by Amazon Italia Logistica S.r.l.
Torrazza Piemonte (TO), Italy

52426553R00025